MY TEENAGE LIFE IN AUSTRALIA

CUSTOMS AND CULTURES OF THE WORLD

MY TEENAGE LIFE IN AUSTRALIA

By Michael Burgan
with Indya Campbell

Series Foreword by
Kum-Kum Bhavnani

MASON CREST

Mason Crest
450 Parkway Drive, Suite D
Broomall, PA 19008
www.masoncrest.com

Printed and bound in the United States of America.

First printing
9 8 7 6 5 4 3 2 1

Series ISBN: 978-1-4222-3899-8
ISBN: 978-1-4222-3900-1
ebook ISBN: 978-1-4222-7879-6

Library of Congress Cataloging-in-Publication Data
Names: Burgan, Michael. | Campbell, Indya, 2000- author.
Title: My teenage life in Australia / by Michael Burgan, with Indya Campbell; series foreword by Kum-Kum Bhavnani.
Description: Broomall, PA : Mason Crest, 2018. | Series: Customs and cultures of the world | Includes index.
Identifiers: LCCN 2017003263| ISBN 9781422239001 (hardback) | ISBN 9781422278796 (ebook)
Subjects: LCSH: Australia--Social life and customs--Juvenile literature. | Teenagers--Australia--Social life and customs--Juvenile literature.
Classification: LCC DU107 .W49 2018 | DDC 305.2350994--dc23
LC record available at https://lccn.loc.gov/2017003263 .

Developed and Produced by Shoreline Publishing Group.
Editor: James Buckley, Jr.
Design: Tom Carling, Carling Design Inc.
Production: Sandy Gordon
www.shorelinepublishing.com

Front cover: Dreamstime.com/Zstockphotos.

QR Codes disclaimer:

You may gain access to certain third party content ("Third-Party Sites") by scanning and using the QR Codes that appear in this publication (the "QR Codes"). We do not operate or control in any respect any information, products, or services on such Third-Party Sites linked to by us via the QR Codes included in this publication, and we assume no responsibility for any materials you may access using the QR Codes. Your use of the QR Codes may be subject to terms, limitations, or restrictions set forth in the applicable terms of use or otherwise established by the owners of the Third-Party Sites. Our linking to such Third-Party Sites via the QR Codes does not imply an endorsement or sponsorship of such Third-Party Sites, or the information, products, or services offered on or through the Third-Party Sites, nor does it imply an endorsement or sponsorship of this publication by the owners of such Third-Party Sites.

 AUSTRALIA

CONTENTS

Key Icons to Look For

 Words to Understand: These words with their easy-to-understand definitions will increase the reader's understanding of the text, while building vocabulary skills.

 Sidebars: This boxed material within the main text allows readers to build knowledge, gain insights, explore possibilities, and broaden their perspectives by weaving together additional information to provide realistic and holistic perspectives.

 Educational Videos: Readers can view videos by scanning our QR codes, providing them with additional educational content to supplement the text. Examples include news coverage, moments in history, speeches, iconic sports moments, and much more!

 Text-Dependent Questions: These questions send the reader back to the text for more careful attention to the evidence presented here.

 Research Projects: Readers are pointed toward areas of further inquiry connected to each chapter. Suggestions are provided for projects that encourage deeper research and analysis.

 Series Glossary of Key Terms: This back-of-the-book glossary contains terminology used throughout this series. Words found here increase the reader's ability to read and comprehend higher-level books and articles in this field.

AUSTRALIA

SERIES FOREWORD

Culture: Parts = Whole

Culture makes us human.

Many of us think of culture as something that belongs to a person, a group, or even a country. We talk about the food of a region as being part of its culture (tacos, pupusas, tamales, and burritos all are part of our understanding of food from Mexico, and South and Central America).

We might also talk about the clothes as being important to culture (saris in India, kimonos in Japan, hijabs or *gallibayas* in Egypt, or beaded shirts in the Navajo Nation). Imagine trying to sum up "American" culture using just examples like these! Yet culture does not just belong to a person or even a country. It is not only about food and clothes or music and art, because those things by themselves cannot tell the whole story.

Culture is also about how we live our lives. It is about our lived experiences of our societies and of all the worlds we inhabit. And in this series—Customs and Cultures of the World—you will meet young people who will share their experiences of the cultures and worlds they inhabit.

How does a teenager growing up in South Africa make sense of the history of apartheid, the 1994 democratic elections, and of what is happening now? That is as integral to our world's culture as the ancient ruins in Greece, the pyramids of Egypt, the Great Wall of China, the Himalayas above Nepal, and the Amazon rain forests in Brazil.

But these examples are not enough. Greece is also known for its financial uncertainties, Egypt is known for the uprisings in Tahrir Square, China is known for its rapid development of megacities, Australia is known for its amazing animals, and Brazil is known for the Olympics and its football [soccer] team. And there are many more examples for each nation, region, and person, and some of these examples are featured in these books. The question is: How do you, growing up in a particular country, view your own culture? What do you think of as culture? What is your lived experience of it? How do you come to understand and engage with cultures that are not familiar to you? And, perhaps most importantly, why do you/we want to do this? And how does reading about and experiencing other cultures help you understand your own?

It is perhaps a cliché to say culture forms the central core of our humanity and our dignity. If that's true, how do young adults talk about your own cultures? How do you simultaneously understand how people apparently "different" from you live their lives, and engage with their cultures? One way is to read the stories in this series. The "authors" are just like you, even though they live in different places and in different cultures. We communicated with these young writers over the Internet, which has become the greatest gathering of cultures ever. The Internet is now central to the culture of almost everyone, with young people leading the way on how to use it to expand the horizons of all of us. From those of us born in earlier generations, thank you for opening that cultural avenue!

Let me finish by saying that culture allows us to open our minds, think about worlds different from the ones we live in, and to imagine how people very different from us live their lives. This series of books is just the start of the process, but a crucial start.

I hope you enjoy them.

—Kum-Kum Bhavnani
Professor of sociology and feminist and global studies at the University of California, Santa Barbara, and an award-winning international filmmaker.

MEET INDYA!

To: The Reader

Subject: About Me!

My name is Indya Meg Campbell. I was born on 12 April 2000 in a town called Wollongong. It's located in the state of New South Wales, which is on the east coast of Australia. The capital city of New South Wales is Sydney and Wollongong is located approximately 80 kilometres (50 miles) south of Sydney. I was born and have lived in Wollongong my whole life.

Wollongong!

AUSTRALIA

My current hobbies are dancing, jazz and hip hop. I used to compete in dancing and cheerleading and was lucky enough to go to Florida in 2014 to compete in an international team competition.

I also like to go the beach in summer. The beach is only about 2 kilometres (1.2 miles) from my home so I am lucky to live so close. Wollongong has beautiful beaches.

Greetings from Wollongong

MEET INDYA

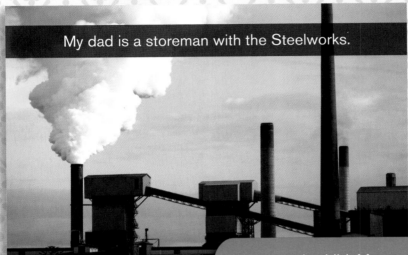

My dad is a storeman with the Steelworks.

I am an only child. My parents separated when I was six years old. They are both single parents and work full time. Both the University and the Steelworks are major industries in Wollongong and employ a large number of people in Wollongong.

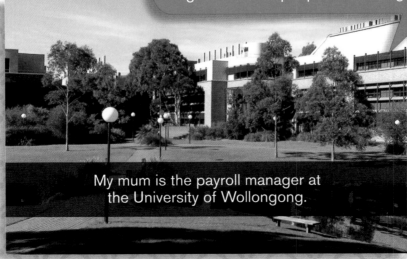

My mum is the payroll manager at the University of Wollongong.

My mum is an only child like me. My Nan and Pop [grandparents] live very close to me in Wollongong and helped bring me up when I was younger. My Nan is from a large family of three brothers and two sisters and most of the extended family also live in Wollongong and surrounding suburbs. We try and all get together a few times during the year but always spend Christmas night together. There are about 30 of the extended family and we have lots of fun and laughs together and all get on very well. We are a nice family.

My dad was born in Dunedin, which is in the South Island of New Zealand. Dad is one of five children and is the only one from his family that lives in Australia. His family has been to visit several times and we have also been to New Zealand for visits. I wouldn't say I have a strong bond with my New Zealand family, but I do have a connection with them and we get along well when we see each other.

I believe family is a big part of my life. They all have done things for me that make me the person I am at 16. My mum, dad, Nan, and Pop have played a big role in my life. They are always there for me through the good and bad times.

Although I mightn't see my extended family a lot I know that they are all close to me and will always be there for me. They are people I can reach out to for anything.

Australia: An Introduction

To many people around the world, Australia is the land of kangaroos and koala bears, where residents and tourists alike romp on any of thousands of beaches. But Australia is also one of the richest countries in the world, with vast deposits of natural resources that it sells overseas. It's also a diverse country. While once a British colony, today many "Aussies" trace their roots to nations around the world. The **indigenous** people of the continent, known as Aboriginal Australians, play a big part, too. The original Australians include a distinct group known as Torres Straits Islanders, who come from islands that lie between Australia and New Guinea to the north.

Words to Understand

contiguous   connected along a border or point

indigenous   native to a particular region, especially referring to people

marsupial   a type of mammal, such as kangaroos, that have a pouch in which mothers carry and feed their babies

nomadic   referring to people that move often to find hunting grounds and places to live

penal colony   an island or other isolated territory where large numbers of prisoners are kept

Australia is divided into six states, plus two major territories, each of which has its own governing body, much like the United States.

Australia is the smallest of the world's seven continents, though it is also Earth's largest island. With an area of 2,969,907 square miles (7.6 million sq km), Australia is the world's sixth-largest country—about the size of the 48 **contiguous** United States. Islands form part of this territory. The most important of these is Tasmania, which is one of Australia's six states. The other states are New South Wales, Victoria, Queensland, Western Australia, and South Australia. The country also includes the Northern Territory and the Capital Territory of Canberra.

AUSTRALIA

Australia is the flattest continent, and the driest after Antarctica. Large parts of Australia's interior are made up of desert, and just a small portion of the country is suitable for growing crops. Australia's major cities ring its long coastline on the Indian, Southern, and South Pacific Oceans. About 80 percent of the country's roughly 24 million people live within 60 miles (96 km) of the shore. Australia's longest river, the Murray, is just over 1,500 miles (2,414 km) long and flows through parts of Victoria, New South Wales, and South Australia.

The Murray River flows through southeastern Australia and includes several placid sections popular with boaters.

Given Australia's size, the people deal with a variety of climates, with hot and dry weather typical in the interior, and colder and wetter weather in the south. Some northern areas are tropical, with high humidity and more rainfall. The continent's extreme weather and barren landscape made living in Australia challenging for the immigrants who began arriving in the 18th century, but the people have prospered.

Aboriginal Australia

Modern scientists and historians think the first humans reached Australia more than 50,000 years ago, though the Aboriginal people say they have always lived on the continent. Some of the early Australians came from Asia and nearby islands by sea, while others crossed land bridges that once connected islands in the region.

The original Aboriginal Australians were mostly **nomadic**, hunting animals, collecting shellfish, and gathering wild crops for food. Their population on the entire continent was never more than one million, and probably closer to half of that. They lived in tribes that numbered from several hundred to several thousand people. Tribes were split into smaller groups of people related to each other. The whole tribe owned the land where the people lived, and tribes often used natural markers, such as rivers, to show the boundaries of their land. At times, tribes clashed over who could hunt in specific areas.

European Discovery

During the late 15th century, Europe entered what is sometimes called its Age of Discovery, as the richest nations began sending ships around the world. The rulers of those nations were looking for gold and other valuable natural resources they could trade for or simply take. The Netherlands set up trading operations in what is now Indonesia. On one journey there in

Tasman's Land

Several decades after Dirk Hartog's voyage to Australia, the Dutch explorer Abel Tasman spotted an island southeast of the main continent. He named it for a Dutch official called Antonie van Diemen. When the British landed on Van Diemen's Land in 1803, it became their second Australian penal colony. The next year, they founded Hobart, the continent's second-oldest city. While the British fought with Aboriginal people across Australia, their treatment of the natives of Van Diemen's Land was especially harsh. During the "black wars" that started in 1828, the British wiped out almost all of the island's native population, with disease killing many as well. By the 1850s, the island was no longer a penal colony, and residents decided to change its name to Tasmania. As with the rest of Australia, Tasmania has wildlife found nowhere else on Earth, such as the **marsupial** called the Tasmanian devil.

1616, Dutch sea captain Dirk Hartog became the first European to land in Australia, reaching an island off the western shore now named for him. The Dutch called the territory New Holland. Australia's modern name comes from a Latin word meaning "southern."

Ships from other European nations sailed close by the western coast of Australia, but it took until 1770 for a European to come ashore on the eastern side of the continent. James Cook led a British expedition that landed in what is now Sydney's Botany Bay. He and his men were amazed by plants and wildlife they had never seen before in Europe or on their travels in the Pacific Ocean.

In 1788, Great Britain decided to send some of its convicted criminals to live and work in Australia. The so-called First Fleet of 11 British ships landed in Botany Bay but soon moved to another spot near a harbor that looked more promising for starting a **penal colony**. There, about 1,500 people built what would become Australia's first permanent English settlement. About half of them were convicts, both men and women. Most of the rest were guards, along with their families.

This artwork shows the arrival from England of the First Fleet to Botany Bay on Australia's southeastern coast. The area today is the city of Sydney.

The arrival of the newcomers led to conflict with the Aboriginal people, with fighting going on for decades. The British, though, with better weapons and eventually more people, took control. The native Australians lost their land, and many also died of disease.

Becoming a Modern Nation

Through the 19th century, the British sent more people to Australia. The colony was built by convicts, people who served their prison term and remained there, and free people seeking a new life in a new land. Some Australians raised sheep and cattle, while farming went on in areas with good soil and enough rain.

A massive gold rush in the early 1850s brought people from around the world to Australia, where they set up temporary camps while mining.

Great Britain stopped sending convicts to New South Wales in 1842. In 1851, thousands of people flocked to Australia after gold was discovered, and other gold rushes followed. Through the century, the British explored more of the continent's interior and established new cities. The wealth from gold helped turn Sydney and Melbourne into modern cities that rivaled those in Europe and North America.

Under British rule, Australia included several separate colonies. In 1901, the colonies merged into one independent nation, though they kept close ties to the "mother" country. Even today, Australia recognizes the British king or queen as its head of state, though not its government.

Because of those ties, Australia sent troops to help Great Britain fight World Wars I and II. In the second war, Australia was directly threatened by Japan, and it relied on US forces to help defend it. That began an enduring relationship with America.

Postwar Growth

After World War II ended, Australia wanted to strengthen its economy, and it welcomed immigrants to help with that task. People from across Europe and other regions made the long voyage to Australia, adding new cultures and customs to what had been largely a British society. (Chinese people, though, had been there since the Gold Rush days.) The newcomers joined Australians in working in factories, mining for such natural resources as iron, copper, and gold, and running shops and restaurants. The government also funded a huge project to generate electricity from water in the Snowy Mountains and nearby rivers. Completed over 25 years, this Snowy Mountains Scheme was the country's largest engineering project ever. It also provided irrigation for farming.

Building the dams, tunnels, and power stations for the plan showed Australia's "can-do" spirit. The country and its leaders were determined to keep Australia moving forward. Still, Australia has not avoided the effects of terrorism common in North America, Europe, and the Middle East, and it still faces other challenges (see The Future of Australia). Despite that, most Australians are satisfied with their country and their lives. ✳

Australia in the 2000s

INDYA'S SCHOOL LIFE

To: **The Reader**

Subject: **My School Life**

I attend an all-girls, private, Catholic school in Wollongong named St Mary's Star of the Sea College. It is a large school, with 1,200 girls. School starts at 8:45 am and ends at 3:15 pm. Our school is all about three morals and demonstrating them within the college. These include: Respect, Responsibility, and Relationships. The school teaches us that if we display responsibility and show respect, then we will create a pleasant and happy environment.

The good thing about the school is that it's right on the beach, making it handy for us on extremely hot days as we can go down to the beach when we finish. With so many girls within the school it is quite busy around the corridors, especially in between classes, usually causing rivalry between different years—ha!

St. Mary's students spelled out NO to protest domestic violence.

To: **The Reader**

Subject: **My School Life**

When we begin senior school ... ...riority is on our studies and school work, so we no longer do sport o... ...in the school. We have 'free' periods instead and these are supposed to be ...udy time.

As I now approach year 12, it becomes a stressful time, with everyone drowning in study. Year 12 is the final year of school before we graduate and perhaps attend University.

My subjects include Standard English; 2 units of Religion, Society, and Culture; PDHPE (Personal Development, Health and Physical Education); CAFS (Community and Family Studies); and Business Services. I chose these subjects, because I was interested in them and felt like they were my strongest subjects. I find that PDHPE is extremely hard with lots of content to it. There is a lot to remember and revise. CAFS to me is an easier subject as it is about current topics and values of society.

At the end of 2017 I will sit for my Higher School Certificate (HSC). I will do exams in all my subjects. These exams are set by the New South Wales Board of Studies, so all schools do the same exams for each subject. We then get a mark and a ranking for each subject. If we do well enough at school, we might get into University and do further studies.

AUSTRALIA

TIME TO EAT!

 New Post

 Indya Meg Campbell
My Favorite Foods
Like • Comment • Share

I love food! I enjoy most cuisines such as Chinese, Thai, Mexican, Vietnamese, and Italian. My friends and I will usually go out on special occasions and like to try different restaurants. There are lots of restaurants in Wollongong and new ones open all the time.

Each morning before school, my friends and I will usually go out for coffee near our school. My favorite breakfast is smashed avocado and feta cheese on toast topped with poached eggs.

For lunch I take something from home. It might be tinned [canned] tuna and crackers, a salad sandwich or wrap or dinner leftovers. I also take fruit, as I like to eat lots of fruit.

For dinner I like spaghetti bolognese, tacos, steak and salad. I don't really liked cooked vegetables but like them raw. I love ice cream and could eat it every day.

I also like Tim Tams, a yummy chocolate biscuit that is very Australian!

TIM TAMS!

If we get take away [food "to go"] for dinner it tends to be Thai or pizza as both are close to my house. As Australia is a multicultural country, we have so many types of food to choose from.

Australian Culture

Given its historical ties to Great Britain, Australia shares cultural traits with that country. In both countries, drivers use the left side of the road, and cricket and rugby are popular sports. (Each has its roots in England.) Australians can watch a television network devoted to British shows. And English, of course, is the major language in both countries.

But Australia's culture has been shaped by many other factors as well. The first British and Irish newcomers faced hardships as they built a new society on the frontier, which led them to value hard work—and to appreciate their leisure time. Then, with the arrival of immigrants from other parts of the world—particularly southern Europe, the Middle East, and Asia—a new, more distinctly Australian culture emerged. In recent decades, the government has stressed that the country is really a multicultural society, and that has meant preserving and promoting Aboriginal culture as well.

Words to Understand

bushranger   an Australian outlaw of the 19th century who often robbed people traveling through remote areas

frontier   land far away from main areas of population

multicultural   describing the combining and respecting of the cultural backgrounds of different peoples in a society

outback   remote rural lands, especially in Australia

Holding a boomerang in his right hand, an Aboriginal performer makes music on the famous large wind instrument known as a didgeridoo.

Aspects of Aboriginal Culture

The Aboriginal Australians did not leave a written history, and their traditions and customs have been passed on orally and through art. Many Aboriginal Australians follow the traditional beliefs. They are part of the world's oldest surviving civilization and practice the oldest religion. The early tribes shared religious beliefs focused on what is called the Dreaming or Dreamtime, when spiritual beings created Earth and everything on it. These beings still exist in the present, as do the spirits of the Aboriginal people's ancestors. The people also feel a close connection to the land and its wildlife.

The earliest Australians left carvings and paintings of animals, people, spirits, and geometric shapes on rocks all over the continent. This rock art helped to record history and also had religious significance. Today, some Aboriginal artists create similar images using such media as paint and canvas or ceramics, while others might use photography, digital art, or a

Ancient cave paintings provide clues to early life on the Australian continent.

variety of other media to express themselves. Musically, some Aboriginal people still play the didgeridoo, a long, thin wind instrument. Musicians in other parts of the world now play this instrument, too.

The ancient Aboriginals spoke hundreds of different languages, and some Aboriginal names for animals and objects are still used in English today. Kangaroo, for example, is an Aboriginal word. So are boomerang and dingo, which refers to a wild dog found only in Australia. The boomerang, an Aboriginal invention, is used for hunting and for sport. The ones used to hunt do not return to the thrower.

Religion

Since the arrival of the British, different forms of Christianity have been the main religion

"Gone Walkabout"

Living simply and relying on nature for food and clothing, the Aboriginal people developed a deep appreciation of the natural world around them. Aboriginal teenage boys went on walkabouts, solitary trips into the wild. They learned how to survive on their own and to connect with the spirits thought to inhabit nature. Aboriginal people still take long walking journeys in the **outback**, following traditional paths on tribal lands as a way to stay connected with the spirits of their ancestors.

for non-Aboriginal people. A recent census showed that just over 30 percent of Australians belonged to one of several Protestant faiths, and about 25 percent were Roman Catholic. A large number of Australians, however—just over 22 percent—said they had no religion. Much smaller percentages followed Buddhism, Hinduism, Islam, or other faiths.

Food and Clothing

The arrival of immigrants has helped the typical Australians' diet evolve from the typical "meat and potatoes" diet of past years. The Asian influence can be seen in spicy noodle dishes, while the Italians introduced pizza. With their vast coastline, Australians can eat a wide variety of fresh fish and shellfish. In the remote desert areas, known as the bush, Aboriginal people still gather such traditional fruits as desert berries and quandongs, and many wind up in restaurants and markets in the country's cities. The people of the bush also hunt such animals as kangaroo and emu for their meat. For dessert, a cake made with meringue and fruit called a pavlova is a popular dish across the country. Another popular local food is vegemite, a spread made by combining yeast left over after brewing beer with spices and some vegetables. While many Aussies love it, foreign visitors usually find it's an acquired taste.

Indya on Faith

Growing up with a Catholic background, you could say I am religious. I follow the Catholic teachings but am not a practicing Catholic in that I don't go to Mass every week. My family and I go to church each Christmas Eve to say our blessings. As I attended a Catholic primary and high school, the whole school comes together for a liturgy or Mass on Easter and Christmas. At primary school we usually came together in the school church each Friday. We have our studies of religion class most days of the week, in which we learn more about our own religious background. I study religion at school and especially like learning about other religions. I find this interesting as I can get a closer insight into the beliefs of others.

For most Australians, their clothing is the same as North Americans and European wear, though some ethnic groups may wear clothing from their native lands on special occasions, such as religious ceremonies. Clothing is often influenced by climate and geography. In the bush, for example, people often wear hats to protect themselves from the sun and tough clothes that will withstand hard working conditions. In beach communities, swimwear is part of life. That includes flip-flops for the feet, colorful shirts, and shorts.

The Fine Arts and Literature

For many years, Australians talked about their "cultural cringe." Many believed their arts and other aspects of culture did not match what was produced in Europe and North America. Now, though, most Australians rightly take pride in what their artists achieve.

The epic novels of Patrick White brought the land and people of Australia to life and helped the world learn more about his nation.

In literature, Patrick White took the world's highest honors for writers when he won the Nobel Prize in 1973 for such novels as *The Tree of Man* and *The Solid Mandala*. More recently, in 2014 Richard Flanagan won the Man Booker prize, a major literary award for books in English, for *The Narrow Road to the Deep North*. Also highly regarded is Thea Astley, who won several Australian literary awards for her fiction.

Sidney Nolan often includes this stark, simplified depiction of Ned Kelly in his paintings about Australian history.

In classical music, Joan Sutherland was one of the 20th century's greatest opera singers. One of the theaters in the Sydney Opera House is named for her. Also winning wide acclaim was Nellie Melba, who appears on the country's $100 bill.

Australian painters often copied styles from abroad, though today's Aboriginal painters use traditional styles to create art found in museums and galleries. Outside of Australia, one of the country's best-known painters is Sidney Nolan, who often painted images inspired by Ned Kelly, a **bushranger** of the 19th century. Kelly has often been a character in plays, poems, and stories.

Hugh Jackman has become world famous as the X-Man called Wolverine in a series of movies. Nicole Kidman has been nominated for four Oscars, winning once.

Popular Arts

Australians have also made their mark in popular culture, with their movies and music popular around the world. Film actors originally from the country include Hugh Jackman, Chris Hemsworth, and Nicole Kidman. The filmmaker George Miller created the Mad Max series of movies in Australia, and actor Paul Hogan played Crocodile Dundee in several movies that brought a taste of Australia to the world.

In popular music, Australia has produced several international stars, including the Bee Gees, Olivia Newton-John, Sia, Nick Cave, Keith Urban, and INXS.

Sports

As part of their "work hard/play hard" approach to life, Australians take part in and watch a number of sports. On an island, water sports are bound to be popular, and Australians have excelled at sailing and especially swimming. The country has produced many swimmers who have won medals at the Summer Olympics, including Ian Thorpe and Leisel Jones. Australia has also twice hosted the Games, in 1956 and 2000. Australians enjoy cricket, rugby, and a form of rugby developed in the country called Australian Rules football. Despite its overall warm, dry climate, some of Australia's mountains in the south get snow, giving people the chance to ski and snowboard. Australia is the only country from the Southern Hemisphere to have won a gold medal at the Winter Olympics. While basketball and baseball are not hugely popular in Australia, several athletes in those sports have gone on to professional careers in North America. Lauren Jackson became a star in the Women's National Basketball Association, and several men play important roles for teams in the National Basketball Association. More than two dozen Australians have played Major League Baseball. ✳

Cricket is one of Australia's favorite sports. Its national team won the 2015 Cricket World Cup, which was played "Down Under."

INDYA'S TOWN

To: The Reader

Subject: My Town

Up until I was 6 years old, I lived in a house with my mum and dad. After their marriage ended, mum and I moved into a townhouse in West Wollongong. It is a 3-bedroom townhouse and I have my own bathroom. We have lived at this location for 9 years. There are 9 townhouses in our block but it is very quiet and we don't see the neighbors very often. When we see each other we wave or have quick conversations.

My dad lives in a 2-bedroom flat in a suburb called Corrimal. It is a ten-minute drive from Wollongong. It is also a quiet neighborhood, but unfortunately there have been a few car accidents on my dad's street that have resulted in two people passing away.

I do share care with my parents. One week I stay with my mum and the other week I stay with my dad. This makes it easier for me to spend quality time with both my parents.

Both areas I live in are suburban areas with houses, units, flats [apartments], schools and shopping centers. I also have access to both bus and trains.

To: **The Reader**

Subject: **My Town**

Wollongong is located between the mountains and the sea. I recommend anyone who wishes to travel to Wollongong to definitely visit all our pretty beaches as they are extremely nice! I think we have some of the best beaches in the world right on our doorstep.

I would also recommend bushwalking on our mountains, viewing from our mountain lookouts, and a walk along the Sea Cliff Bridge. The Nan Tien Temple (left) and Symbio Wildlife Park (right) are also great to visit.

Sea Cliff Bridge

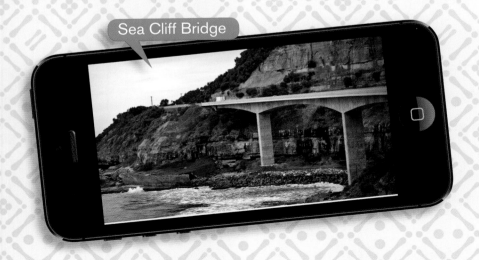

Australian Customs

A man entering an Australian shop or running into a friend on the street is likely to be greeted with "G'day, mate." This greeting comes from a tradition in which one's "mates" were the people they could count on most when they needed help. Now, the custom of casually calling someone a mate is sometimes even applied to women, and the phrase "G'day, mate" is one many English speakers around the world associate with Australia.

Despite having diverse ethnic backgrounds, Australians are united in part by their language, though some of its "English" words might sound foreign to American ears. Australians often shorten common words, and the most famous example may be using *barbie* for *barbecue*. *Fair dinkum* is another expression non-Australians might recognize, used to describe something or someone that is honest or true.

Words to Understand

memorial   describing events held to honor the dead

secular   referring to things not associated with a religion or its beliefs

Southern Hemisphere   the half of the world that lies south of the Equator

Religious Holidays

If language is one thing that unifies Australians, so are the national holidays. Settled by Europeans who followed the teachings of different Christian faiths, Christmas is an important holiday for most Australians, and even non-Christians enjoy the time off and the festivities. But since Australia is in the **Southern Hemisphere**, the seasons are reversed compared to North America, so Christmas comes in the middle of summer. That means Australians can enjoy an outdoor meal or a swim at the beach after they open presents. Following British custom, Australians also celebrate Boxing Day, December 26, when people traditionally visited friends to exchange gifts. Two other important dates

Barbies and Shouts

"Bring a plate," someone just invited to a barbecue might hear from the host. But that doesn't mean to bring a dish to eat off of—it means guests should bring their own food to toss on the grill (below) or some other dish to share. Australians are not offended when asked to contribute in this way, though they would not likely ask a foreign guest to do so. The guest, however, would earn points by bringing wine—made at one of Australia's many wineries— or beer. Another tradition at gatherings in a pub (bar) is shouting. That doesn't mean to yell out loud, but to offer to buy a round a drinks for everyone in a group. Leaving friends without shouting is considered bad manners, and social standing doesn't come into play—everyone is expected to shout, from the wealthiest member of the group to the least well-off.

Members of the Australian Navy march in an Anzac Day parade, a memorial holiday honoring the military of Australia and New Zealand.

to Christians, Good Friday and Easter, are also marked as national holidays. Individual states and territories also declare their own holidays. Members of non-Christian faiths also celebrate the holidays important to their religions.

Secular Holidays

Some of the most important secular Australian holidays mark important events in the country's history. April 25 is Anzac Day and honors Australians who have died in battle. The date is the anniversary of when Australian and New Zealand soldiers, collectively known as ANZAC, came ashore at Gallipoli, Turkey, in 1915 during World War I. In cities and towns across the country, military veterans march and hold memorial services to honor the dead, and whole communities take part. During the ceremonies, one custom is to read lines from the poem "For the Fallen" by Lawrence Binyon. The words stress that the living will always remember the sacrifices of the soldiers killed in battle.

The other major national secular holiday is Australia Day, January 26. That marks the day in 1788 when the First Fleet reached Sydney Harbor. It was first celebrated in that city and became a public holiday for all of New South Wales in 1818. Today, Australians everywhere mark the day with a variety of festivities, from concerts and boat races to public meals and fireworks. The night before Australia Day, the government announces the winners of the Australian of Year in several categories, honoring people who have made important contributions to the country on both the national and state/territorial level.

Australia Day is the country's national holiday and is celebrated with parades, parties, and enormous fireworks displays.

Though Australia mostly has a very warm climate, there is skiing at some high elevations, such as these slopes at Perisher Valley near Canberra.

New Year's Day is another national holiday, and Australians welcome in the New Year with fireworks and parties. Given its geographic location, Sydney is one of the first major cities in the world to celebrate New Year's, and it's known for the huge party that goes on around its famous Opera House in the harbor.

Showing Australia's ongoing connection to Great Britain, all the states and territories also celebrate the birthday of the British monarch, though the date varies. Most states celebrate it in June. Since 1952, when Queen Elizabeth took power, the day has been called the Queen's Birthday, but that will change when a king takes the throne. While this holiday doesn't have the same ceremonies that fill Anzac and Australia Days, Australians do appreciate the day off, which many use to hit the country's ski slopes, located mostly in Victoria and New South Wales. On that day, the monarch also announces the names of people chosen to receive honors from the British government. Not everyone likes the Queen's Birthday, however. People who oppose Australia's continuing political ties to Great Britain would rather honor someone else on that day or get rid of it all together. ✳

Celebrate Australia Day!

INDYA'S FREE TIME

To: The Reader

Subject: My Free Time

I have attended the NRG Dance School for nine years. It is a great dance school with wonderful teachers and students. I have made so many great friends through dancing. For eight years I danced competitively in a team. We did jazz, hip hop, contemporary and modern dances. I also competed in cheerleading for seven years. My dancing has taken me interstate to compete and also to America. We competed at "Worlds" in 2014 and it was held in Florida. My team was lucky enough to come seventh in the world in our junior jazz section. A great result for a small Australian dance school!

On my American trip we also visited Los Angeles, New York, Las Vegas and Hawaii. It is a trip I will always remember as I had a great time and was with awesome dance families.

To: The Reader

Subject: My Music

Just being around my friends is great, no matter what we are doing and what our plans bring us. I also enjoy just listening to music on my own when I'm feeling like I need my own space and I just want to chill out. I like most modern music and also like some old stuff. I don't like country and western music or opera. It is good to just listen to music and sing and dance around.

When I am in my own bubble I like listening to in particular, Kid Ink, which is one of my all time favorite singers/rappers.

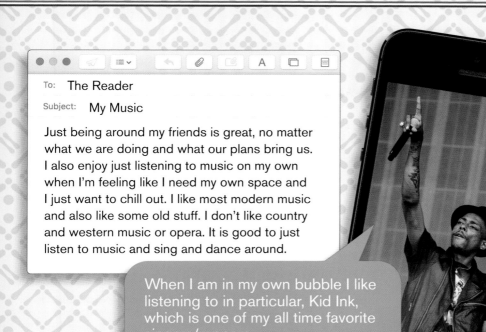

To: The Reader

Subject: My Travels

I really like to travel and have been lucky enough to go overseas. I have been to New Zealand several times, Bali four times (right), Thailand twice, Fiji, and America. I have also traveled a little bit in Australia and have been to Queensland and Victoria. Australia is such a big country that it takes a long time to get anywhere. Most trips interstate you have to fly because driving takes so long.

Australia's Economy and Politics

Australia ranks as one of the world's largest economies, measured by **gross domestic product**. In 2016, its GDP was more than $1.3 trillion (measured in US dollars). Australia's economy has grown every year for almost three decades—something no other country in the world can claim. The unemployment rate was under six percent in 2016, meaning most Australians who want to work can find a job. Inflation is low, meaning the cost of goods and services does not rise much each year. The cost of buying a home, though, has gone up in recent years, and people who live in the major cities often have to live outside the city and commute.

Words to Understand

amended   made a change to a legal document

coalition   a group of two or more political parties that jointly govern a nation

gross domestic product   the total value of the goods and services a country produces

monarchy   a government ruled by a king or queen

The world-famous Sydney Opera House is the centerpiece of Sydney Harbor. The building is designed to look like shark teeth.

The Main Sectors of the Economy

In 2016, almost 60 percent of the country's economic activity was in the service sector. This includes such things as banking, insurance, retail sales, transportation, education, tourism, and medical care. Tourism has grown in recent years, fueled in part by an increase in visitors from China. Popular attractions include the Great Barrier Reef, which stretches for more than 1,400 miles and features the world's largest system of coral reefs. Tourists also enjoy visiting Uluru, or Ayers Rock, a massive rock formation that rises more than 1,100 feet above the desert floor in the Northern Territory. The site is sacred to the Anangu, the Aboriginal people who run the national park that surrounds Uluru.

The Underground Town

Coober Pedy calls itself the opal capital of the world. It provides most of the opals used in the world's jewelry. This town in South Australia also attracts tourists curious about how people live there. Many residents live in what are called dugouts. Originally these were holes left behind in the side of hills as miners searched for opals. The dugouts stayed cool during the region's brutally hot summers and were warm during the desert's cool winter nights. Today, the underground homes contain modern appliances, and new dugouts are created using tunneling machines. Visitors can stay in underground motels and guesthouses, and Coober Pedy even has a church that's underground.

The next largest sector is industry, which includes the manufacturing of goods and the extracting of natural resources. The number of manufacturing jobs has shrunk over the last few decades, as companies find it cheaper to make goods in China and other parts of Asia. But Australians still make steel, chemical goods, food products, and other goods.

Australia's huge reserves of gold, copper, and other resources are an important part of its economy. Australia is second only to China in annual gold production and it has more reserves than any other country. But at times the prices for those resources fall, as they did in 2014, and then mining jobs can disappear.

The third major sector of any country's economy is agriculture. While sheep raising has declined in recent years, Australian ranchers have increased their cattle herds. About 90 percent of the country's farmland is used for grazing livestock. Important farm products include wheat, dairy items, a variety of fruits and vegetables, and nuts. Some Australian farmers grow grapes that are turned into wine, and those wines are sold around the world.

Australia's enormous land contains many valuable natural resources. Gold mining is just one of several ways that minerals and elements are extracted for use.

Governing Australia

Australia is a representative democracy—voters choose who will represent them in the government and make the country's laws. The country is also a constitutional **monarchy**. This means the ruler of the United Kingdom is considered the head of state, though he or she plays a limited

Australia's capital is not one of the big coastal cities but comparatively small Canberra. Pictured is the country's parliament building.

role in governing the nation. The monarch is represented in Australia by the governor-general, who is chosen by the king or queen. This person has several duties, including giving final approval to laws and commanding the country's military.

Australia has a federal government system, as does the United States, meaning the states and the national government share powers. The nature of the national government is outlined in the country's constitution, which went into effect in 1901, though it has been **amended** several times.

The Federal Government

The national, or federal, government has three branches. The legislative branch, called Parliament, makes laws. Parliament is divided into two branches, the House of Representatives and the Senate. Each state elects 12 senators and each territory elects two, for a total of 76. The House currently has 150 members, and the number from each state and territory is based on its population. The political party or **coalition** that controls the most votes in the House selects the prime minister, who is the head of the government. The leading parties in Australia are the Liberal Party, the Nationals, and the Labor Party.

As well as being a lawmaker, the prime minister is in charge of the executive branch, which carries out the laws passed in Parliament. The prime minister selects a member of his party or coalition in Parliament to serve as the head of different executive departments. Together, these department ministers form what is called a Cabinet. Some of these departments include Foreign Affairs, Defense, Environment and Energy, and Indigenous Affairs.

Key prime ministers in Australia's history include Sir Robert Menzies, who served for over 18 years—longer than any other prime minister. During

In his first stint as prime minister, Sir Robert Menzies helped Australia deal with World War II. After the war, he led an industrial rebirth.

the 1950s and 1960s, he strengthened the country's ties to the United States. Serving second longest was John Howard, from 1996 to 2007. In 2010, Julia Gillard became the country's first female prime minister. She served until 2013. As of 2017, Malcolm Turnbull was prime minister.

The third branch of the federal government is the judiciary. This is Australia's system of courts. The most powerful court is the High Court, which decides if laws violate the constitution. It also hears appeals of lower

Australian prime minister Malcolm Turnbull met in 2016 with Chinese premier Xi Jinping. Australia works hard to have a major presence in Asia and Oceania.

court decisions. Its members are chosen by the governor-general. Once appointed, the judges serve for life or until the age of 70, unless they break the law or are no longer physically able to serve. Below this court are ones that handle such issues as family disputes, tax law, and criminal cases.

State and Territorial Government

The system set up at the federal level is duplicated in Australia's states. Each state has a constitution and a government with legislative, executive, and judicial branches. States pass their own laws but they can't conflict with federal law. The two mainland territories have their own parliaments as well. State and territorial government address such issues as education, public health, and public safety. The states and the Northern Territory also set the powers of the local governments, which are called councils. ✸

Australian politics

INDYA'S COUNTRY

To: The Reader

Subject: My Country

As an Australian citizen, I consider myself being extremely lucky and fortunate. I like to think of it in terms of: We are not a third-world country; we aren't known for having problems and issues such as terrorism attacks and wars, and we are also known for having over 500 pretty national parks that are worth visiting, especially for tourists. What I also like about Australia is that it is made up of diverse cultures and backgrounds meaning it is considered a multicultural country. I usually tend to take what I have for granted and I have come to the realization that I shouldn't. Because I have grown up in a wealthy home, country, and family, I wish for nothing more.

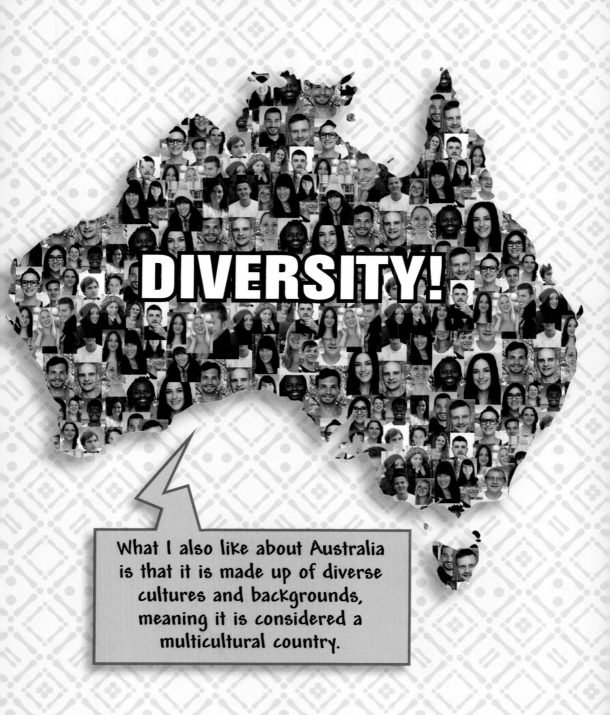

DIVERSITY!

What I also like about Australia is that it is made up of diverse cultures and backgrounds, meaning it is considered a multicultural country.

The Future of Australia

Australia has seen steady economic growth for decades, and Australians enjoy one of the highest standards of living in the world. But the drop in prices for many of its natural resources in 2014 and 2015 showed that the country can still face uncertainty. Events in other countries influence that part of Australia's economy. If worldwide demand for coal or gold drops, Australian producers feel the effects.

In the years to come, Australia will also have to deal with an aging population. By 2030, the government estimates that almost 20 percent of Australians will be 65 or older. Those people will increase the demand for health care and other social services the government provides. Paying for those services could require raising taxes or reducing costs in other parts of the government.

Words to Understand

discrimination   denying people their legal rights because of some personal trait, such as their race or ethnic background

emission   substance, often a gas, released into the air during a chemical or mechanical process

poach   illegally hunt animals that receive government protection

refugee   a person who has fled his or her own country because of war or a national disaster

Australians of all backgrounds take part in Reconciliation Day ceremonies, when Australians of British descent apologize for what was done to Aborigines.

A Diverse Society

Another segment of the population that receives special government attention are the Aboriginal Australians. Their numbers have risen slightly over the last 15 years and now make up about three percent of the population. The government is trying to overcome the mistreatment and **discrimination** the Aboriginal people often faced in the past. For several decades it has returned land taken from them by white settlers. One current goal is to close the economic and social gap between the Aboriginal people and other Australians. One way to do this is to improve education for Aboriginal children. Another is to improve the health of pregnant women and their infants. Part of that includes providing more fresh fruits and vegetables to Aboriginal communities. The effort to "close the gap" will continue in the years ahead.

Terrorist Threat

Some of the people seeking to enter Australia are from the Middle East, which is the home of several terrorist groups. Australia is one of many countries that have been the target of terrorist attacks, most carried out by Australians who claim allegiance to the foreign terrorists. Similar problems are occurring in many Western and European countries. The openness of those societies makes it easier for people to enter, even if they have bad intentions.

A man held several people hostage in a Sydney mall in 2014; two people died in the attack. Australian police have also been able to learn about and prevent some attacks before they occurred, including one at the end of 2016. Terrorism experts, though, believe Australia will continue to face the threat of terrorist attacks, with a growing likelihood that the attackers would come from Asia. In fact, one report placed Australia third behind the United States and Great Britain among countries most likely to be the target of such attacks.

The government has a system that warns people of the possibility of an attack, based on information it has gathered. It tries to balance Australians' safety with their desire to live as freely as possible.

The Challenge of Climate Change

Another challenge Australians confront is climate change. Globally, average temperatures have risen over the last few decades, and scientists predict a continued rise if countries don't reduce the **emission** of greenhouse

Australian special police helped rescue this woman and others during a terrorist-led hostage situation in 2014. Other such attacks have been foiled in the years since.

Protecting the Great Barrier Reef

Even before global warming made the news this century, Australians could see that human activity was damaging the Great Barrier Reef. Fishing, development along the coast, and pollution all played a part. Climate change is just adding to the problem. The reef is a World Heritage site, recognizing its unique natural value. The system of coral reefs is the world's largest living structure. To protect it and the wildlife around it, the governments of Australia and Queensland set up a plan in 2015 to make sure the reef was preserved for decades to come. The steps include prohibiting the development of new ports, cleaning water from land that runs into coastal waters, and increasing penalties for people who try to **poach** wildlife. Taking steps to reduce its emission of greenhouse gases is also part of this plan.

gases, such as carbon dioxide, that contribute to this global warming. Australia has already seen the effects of climate change, with longer and more severe heat waves, changes in average rainfall (both higher and lower that average, depending on the region), and a rise in the sea level. If the seas continue to rise, parts of Australia's coastal cities will face a higher risk of flooding. Warming seas and increased acid in the water could also further damage the Great Barrier Reef.

To help fight climate change, Australia is trying to cut back on the use of fuels, such as coal, that produce greenhouse gases. At the same time, the country is moving to produce more of its energy from "clean" sources.

Australia is trying to be a world leader in production of "green" energy, such as from this wind farm.

The Refugee Issue

Since the end of World War II, Australia has welcomed more than seven million immigrants to the country, but in recent years it has struggled with how to handle **refugees**. These are people fleeing their homeland, often because of war, and then enter Australia's waters on small boats. The

Australia prides itself, for the most part, in its multicultural lifestyle, taking advantage of the many ways that people can contribute to society.

country has sent these people to refugee camps in the nearby countries of Nauru and Papua New Guinea. But that practice draws criticism from people who say the camps don't provide adequate housing and medical care. International aid groups have decried the conditions, calling them some of the worst in the world. Some of the people—mostly men who come from the Middle East and Africa—have been there in limbo for several years. There was a deal with the United States to help settle some of these people, but the Trump administration made early signals that it would revisit that agreement. Meanwhile, Australia is continuing to search for a way to keep control of its borders while still helping refugees. On average, the country takes in more than 10,000 refugees a year.

Moving Forward

Despite the challenges they face, Australians take pride in the democratic ideas that shape their nation. They honor the spirit of hard work that helped them build one of the world's strongest economies. And they strive for harmony in their multicultural society. In 2017, Prime Minister Malcolm Turnbull summed up the feelings of many Australians when he said, "Freedom, diversity, and security—these are great Australian strengths. And they are built upon a foundation of mutual respect." ✳

Refugees and Australia

TEXT-DEPENDENT QUESTIONS

1. How did the original Aboriginal Australians reach the continent?

2. What was the importance of the Snowy Mountain Scheme?

3. What is Anzac Day and how is it usually celebrated?

4. How do Australians often greet each other?

5. What is the capital city of Australia?

6. What distinction does Australia have among countries that compete in the Winter Olympics?

7. Why is climate change a concern to many Australians?

RESEARCH PROJECTS

You can research many fascinating aspects of Australian history and culture. Here are some ideas.

1. The American Revolution played a part in Great Britain's decision to send prisoners to Australia. Research how the events in America shaped that decision.

2. Australia has animals found nowhere else on Earth, such as the platypus and the kangaroo. What happened thousands of years ago to give Australia so many animals that only live on the continent?

3. Ned Kelly is Australia's most famous bushranger and is considered a folk hero. Find out more about his life and explore why some people see him as a hero, even though he was an outlaw.

4. In 1972 Neville Bonner was the first Aboriginal person elected to Australia's Parliament. Linda Burney became the first Aboriginal woman elected to Parliament in 2016. Choose one of these politicians and write a brief report on their lives.

FIND OUT MORE

Books

Aboriginal Rights Movement. Chicago: World Book, 2011.

Perritano, John. *Australia*. Broomall, PA: Mason Crest, 2015.

Woolf, Alex. *Sailing the Great Barrier Reef*. New York: Gareth Stevens Publishing, 2015.

Websites

www.australia.gov.au/about-australia
From the Australian government, a look at the country's history and culture.

ngm.nationalgeographic.com/2013/06/aboriginal-australians/finkel-text
This article from *National Geographic* gives a first-person account of Aboriginal life today.

www.cia.gov/library/publications/the-world-factbook/geos/as.html
CIA World Factbook: Australia
This site gives an overview of Australia, with brief descriptions of its geography, government, economy, people, and more.

www.australia.gov.au/about-australia/our-country/our-natural-environment
Another government site, this one focuses on Australia's geography and wildlife.

SERIES GLOSSARY OF KEY TERMS

arable land   land suitable for cultivation and the growing of crops

commodity   a raw material that has value and is regularly bought and sold

cuisine   cooking that is characteristic of a particular country, region, or restaurant

destabilize   damage, disrupt, undermine

dynasties   long periods of time during which one extended family rules a place

industrialization   the process in which an economy is transformed from mainly agricultural to one based on manufacturing goods

infrastructure   buildings, roads, services, and other things that are necessary for a society to function

lunar calendar   a calendar based on the period from one moon to the next. Each cycle is 28 1/2 to 29 days, so the lunar year is about 354 days

parliamentary   describes a government in which a body of cabinet ministers is chosen from the legislature and act as advisers to the chief of state (or prime minister)

resonate   echo and reverberate; stay current through time

sovereignty   having supreme power and authority

venerate   treat with great respect

INDEX

Photo Credits

Adobe Images: Natasa Tatarin 11, olive1976 13. AP Images/Rob Griffith 55. AStar: 28. Dreamstime.com: David May 9, Martingraf 10t, Kerry Whitelegg 14, Johncarnemolla 16, Syda Productions 21, Vladislav Nosik 22t, Anna1311 22c, Inga Nielsen 22b, Sommai Sommai 23b, Showface 23t, Rozenn Leard 25, 53, Ecophoto 26, Laurence Agron 30, Mitchell Gunn 31, Danemo 32, Phper 33l, Lydia 33r, creativefire 35, Gigsy2222 36, David Steele 37, Volodymyr Vyshnivetskyy 38m, Alexei Averianov 41b, Bhauxwell 43, Zstockphotos 45, Dan Breckwoldt 46, Pepinilla 50, Boarding1now 51, Tanya Puntti 56, Flowertime 57, Rawpixelimages 58. Christopher Chan: 20. Newscom: Dafydd Owen/Photoshot 41t; Ma Zhancheng/UPI 48. Wikimedia: Bilby 23t, TimK13 33r. Wikiwand: 10b, 17, 18.

Author

Michael Burgan has written more than 250 books for children and teens, as well as newspaper articles and blog posts. Although not an athlete, he has written on both amateur and professional sports, including books on the Basketball Hall of Fame, the Olympics, and great moments in baseball. And although not a medical professional, he regularly writes web content on a variety of health topics. He lives in Santa Fe, New Mexico with his cat Callie. (Thanks to Megan Serrano for her help in connecting us with Indya.)